CH0040S861

Andrew Carter

Anthems

10 anthems for mixed voices

MUSIC DEPARTMENT

OXFORD
UNIVERSITY PRESS

OXFORD
UNIVERSITY PRESS

Great Clarendon Street, Oxford OX2 6DP, England
198 Madison Avenue, New York, NY10016, USA

Oxford University Press is a department of the University of Oxford.
It furthers the University's aim of excellence in research, scholarship,
and education by publishing worldwide

Oxford is a registered trade mark of Oxford University Press
in the UK and in certain other countries

© Oxford University Press 2002

The moral rights of the author have been asserted
Database right Oxford University Press (maker)

This collection first published 2002

All rights reserved. No part of this publication may be reproduced,
stored in a retrieval system, or transmitted, in any form or by any means,
without the prior permission in writing of Oxford University Press,
or as expressly permitted by law. Enquiries concerning reproduction
outside the scope of the above should be sent to the Music Copyright
Department, Oxford University Press, at the address above

Permission to perform the works in this anthology in public
(except in the course of divine worship) should normally be obtained
from the Performing Right Society Ltd. (PRS), 29/33 Berners Street,
London W1T 3AB, or its affiliated Societies in each country throughout
the world, unless the owner or the occupier of the premises
being used holds a licence from the Society

Permission to make a recording must be obtained in advance
from the Mechanical Copyright Protection Society Ltd. (MCPS),
Elgar House, 41 Streatham High Road, London SW16 1ER,
or its affiliated Societies in each country throughout the world

1 3 5 7 9 10 8 6 4 2

ISBN 0-19-353087-2

Music origination by Barnes Music Engraving Ltd., East Sussex
Printed in Great Britain on acid-free paper by
Caligraving Ltd., Thetford, Norfolk.

Contents

God be in my head   4

The Light of the World   8

Go before us, O Lord   16

Dear Lord and Father   18

The Lord is my shepherd   24

Deep Peace   35

Mary's Magnificat   40

An Affirmation   44

May the mystery of God enfold us   46

Rejoice in the Lord alway   52

For Julian and Mandy

God be in my head

Book of Hours, Sarum, 1514

ANDREW CARTER

Also available separately: E159; ISBN 0-19-351145-2

This piece © Oxford University Press 1992 and 2002.
This collection © Oxford University Press 2002.

Printed in Great Britain.
OXFORD UNIVERSITY PRESS, MUSIC DEPARTMENT, GREAT CLARENDON STREET, OXFORD OX2 6DP

Photocopying this copyright material is ILLEGAL.

Bishopthorpe, YORK
May 1991

For Steven Jobman and the Chancel Choir of the
First United Presbyterian Church, Galesburg, Illinois, USA.
Commissioned for the installation of Norman E. Myer as Pastor, 1988.

The Light of the World

Revelation 3:20
John 8:12, 10:11, 14:6, 11:25

ANDREW CARTER

Also available separately: E161; ISBN 0–19–351147–9

Duration: 5 mins.

© Oxford University Press 1994 and 2002. Photocopying this copyright material is ILLEGAL.

said,   I am the good

shep - - herd: that_____

giv-eth his life   for the sheep.

Je - sus said,

Ped. 16'

Bishopthorpe, YORK
Holy Week 1988

In memory of Grace Frankell

Go before us, O Lord

Adapted from the Book of Common Prayer

ANDREW CARTER

Words in italics are the original Book of Common Prayer text.

Duration: 1' 35''

Also available separately: E167; ISBN 0–19–351154–1

© Oxford University Press 2000 and 2002. Photocopying this copyright material is ILLEGAL.

Bishopthorpe, YORK
15 July 1998

Dear Lord and Father

(*Dear loving God*)

John Greenleaf Whittier
(1807–92)

ANDREW CARTER

Second movement of *Song of Stillness* (vocal score ISBN 0–19–335521–3)

© Oxford University Press 1998 and 2002. Photocopying this copyright material is ILLEGAL.

In deep - er rev' - rence praise. In sim - ple
In sim - ple
In sim - ple

trust like theirs who heard be - side the Sy - rian sea The gra - cious
trust
trust like theirs who The

Let us, like them, with - out a word,
call - ing of the Lord, Let us, like them, let us, like
Let us, like them, with - out a word,
call - - - ing of the Lord, Let us, like

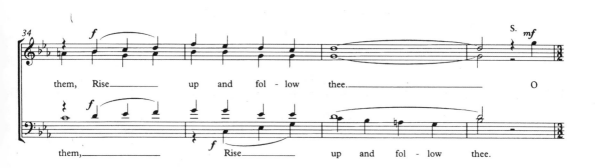

them, Rise up and fol - low thee. O
them, Rise up and fol - low thee.

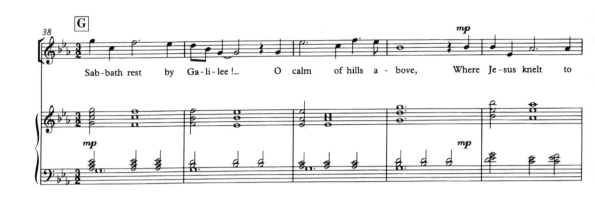

Sab-bath rest by Ga-li-lee!_ O calm of hills a - bove, Where Je -sus knelt to

share with thee The si - - lence of e - ter - - - ni - ty

In - ter - -pre-ted by love!

Drop thy still dews of

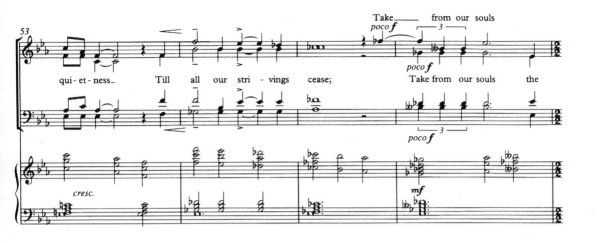

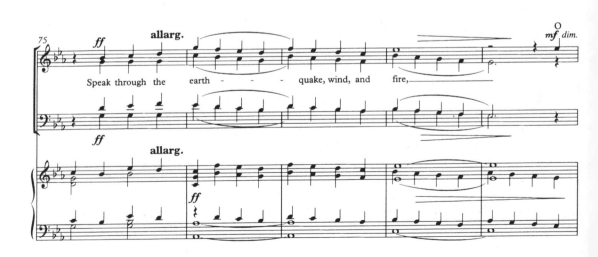

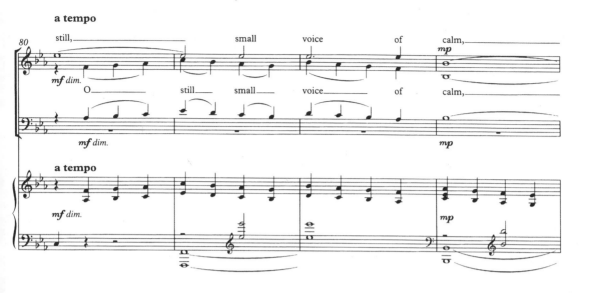

*Commissioned for the installation of Rev. David J. A. Gibbs as
Pastoral Associate at First United Presbyterian Church, Galesburg, Illinois, USA.*

The Lord is my shepherd

Psalm 23

ANDREW CARTER

Also available separately: A415; ISBN 0–19–350466–9

Duration: 6 mins.

© Oxford University Press 1992 and 2002. Photocopying this copyright material is ILLEGAL.

For Mel Olson and the Zephyr Point Church Music Festival, Nevada, 1990

Deep Peace

for choir and congregation

V.1: An old Gaelic blessing
V.2 and 3: Andrew Carter

ANDREW CARTER

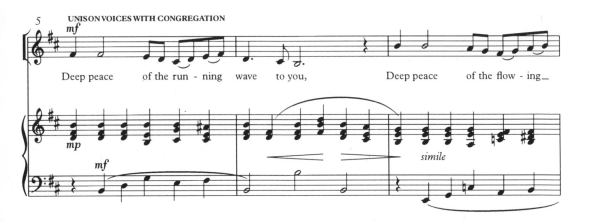

Also available separately: A424; ISBN 0–19–350479–0

Duration: 3′ 30″

© Oxford University Press 1995 and 2002. Photocopying this copyright material is ILLEGAL.

38

Bishopthorpe, YORK
July 1990

For Roy Massey, David Briggs, and Hereford Cathedral Choir

Mary's Magnificat

ANDREW CARTER

Also available separately: X299; ISBN 0–19–353083–X

© Oxford University Press 1986 and 2002. Photocopying this copyright material is ILLEGAL.

King— of— kings.

Solo (Fl. 8' + 4')

mf

(Sw.)

(Ped.)

S. SOLO

mf tranquillo

2. My soul doth mag - ni - fy, doth mag - ni - fy the Lord:

Sw. *mp*

(tacet)

(S. SOLO)

And my spi - rit hath re - joiced,

mp

poco cresc.

mf

Ah _____

mp *poco cresc.* *mf*

re-joiced in God___ my___ Sa - - - viour.

Ah_____ Ah_____

ORGAN

Sw. *mp*

Ped.

3. Ma - ry her song___ to___ Je - sus   Soft - ly, se - rene - ly___ sings:

S.
A.

3. Ma - ry___ her___ song to___ Je - sus   Soft - ly,___ se - rene - ly___ sings:

T.
B.

mp

poco cresc.   *poco forte*

'I will love ___ you, ___ I will serve ___ you, ___ May my lul - la-by glo - ri - fy,

poco cresc.   *poco forte*

In memory of my Godmother, Patricia Caulder

An Affirmation

attrib. Stephen Grellet
(1773–1855) *

ANDREW CARTER

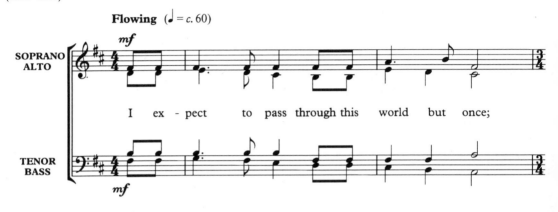

Duration: 1' 25''

* This text had also been attributed to many other people, including Thomas Carlyle and Edward Courtenay, Earl of Essex.

Also available separately: E168; ISBN 0–19–351155–X

© Oxford University Press 2000 and 2002. Photocopying this copyright material is ILLEGAL.

ren - der to a - ny soul_____ of man___ or a - ni-mal,

let me do it now; let me not de - fer___ or ne -

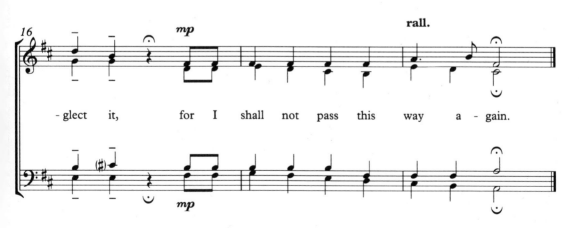

- glect it, for I shall not pass this way a - gain.

Bishopthorpe, YORK
4 August 1998

To Martin Setchell and the Choir of St. Barnabas Church, Fendalton, New Zealand

May the mystery of God enfold us

(A Blessing)

Joy Cowley *   ANDREW CARTER

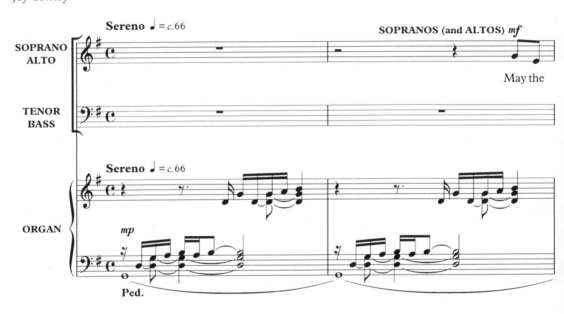

Duration: 2' 30''

* The Arohanui Blessing; from *Psalms Down-Under*; published 1996 by Catholic Supplies, Wellington, New Zealand.

Also available separately: A443; ISBN 0–19–343246–3

Music © Oxford University Press 2001 and 2002.
Text © Joy Cowley 1996
Photocopying this copyright material is ILLEGAL.

wis - dom of God up - hold us, May the

fra - grance of God be a - round us, May the

bright - ness of God sur - round us.

49

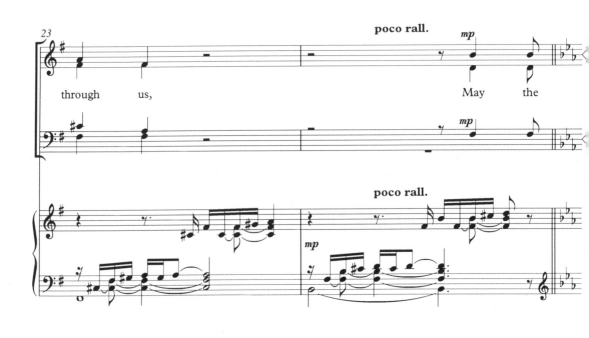

Bishopthorpe, YORK
30 June 1995

For Ian Holiday and the Chapel Choir of Epsom College.
Commissioned for the Founder's Day Service of Thanksgiving: 29 May 1999

Rejoice in the Lord alway

Philippians IV: 4–8

ANDREW CARTER

Also available separately: A445; ISBN 0–19–350499–5

Duration: 5′ 30″

© Oxford University Press 2001 and 2002. Photocopying this copyright material is ILLEGAL.

54

-gain I say, a - gain I say Re - joice.

Ped.

59

mf

65 **Meno mosso** ♩ = 96

BASS SOLO *mf legato*

Be care - ful for

Solo 1

legato mf

mp

70

no-thing; but in ev - 'ry thing by ___ prayer and sup - pli -

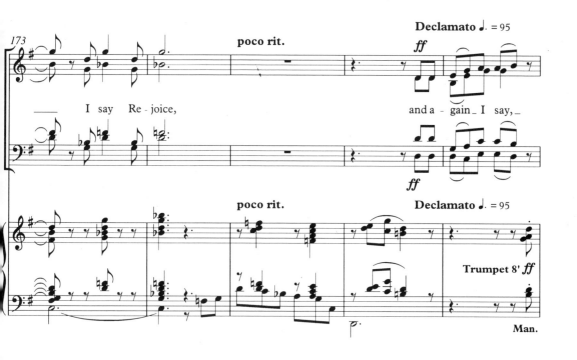

Bishopthorpe, YORK
18 February 1999